Letting Go

Written by: Martin Bissett
Illustrated by: Pamela Carter

Copyright © 2023 by Martin Bissett. All rights reserved.

This book or any portion thereof may not be reproduced or used in any manner whatsoever without the express written permission of the publisher except for the use of brief quotations in a book review.

Strenuous attempts have been made to credit all copyrighted materials used in this book. All such materials and trademarks, which are referenced in this book, are the full property of their respective copyright owners. Every effort has been made to obtain copyright permission for material quoted in this book. Any omissions will be rectified in future editions.

Illustrations by: Pamela Carter
Book design & Publishing Management by: SWATT Books Ltd

Printed in the United Kingdom
First Printing, 2023

ISBN: 978-1-7397421-1-9 (Paperback)

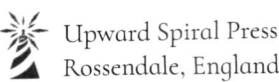

Upward Spiral Press
Rossendale, England

Dedicated to every person
who had to overcome
the opinions of authority
figures, in order to
become their best selves.

Time is like a dream.

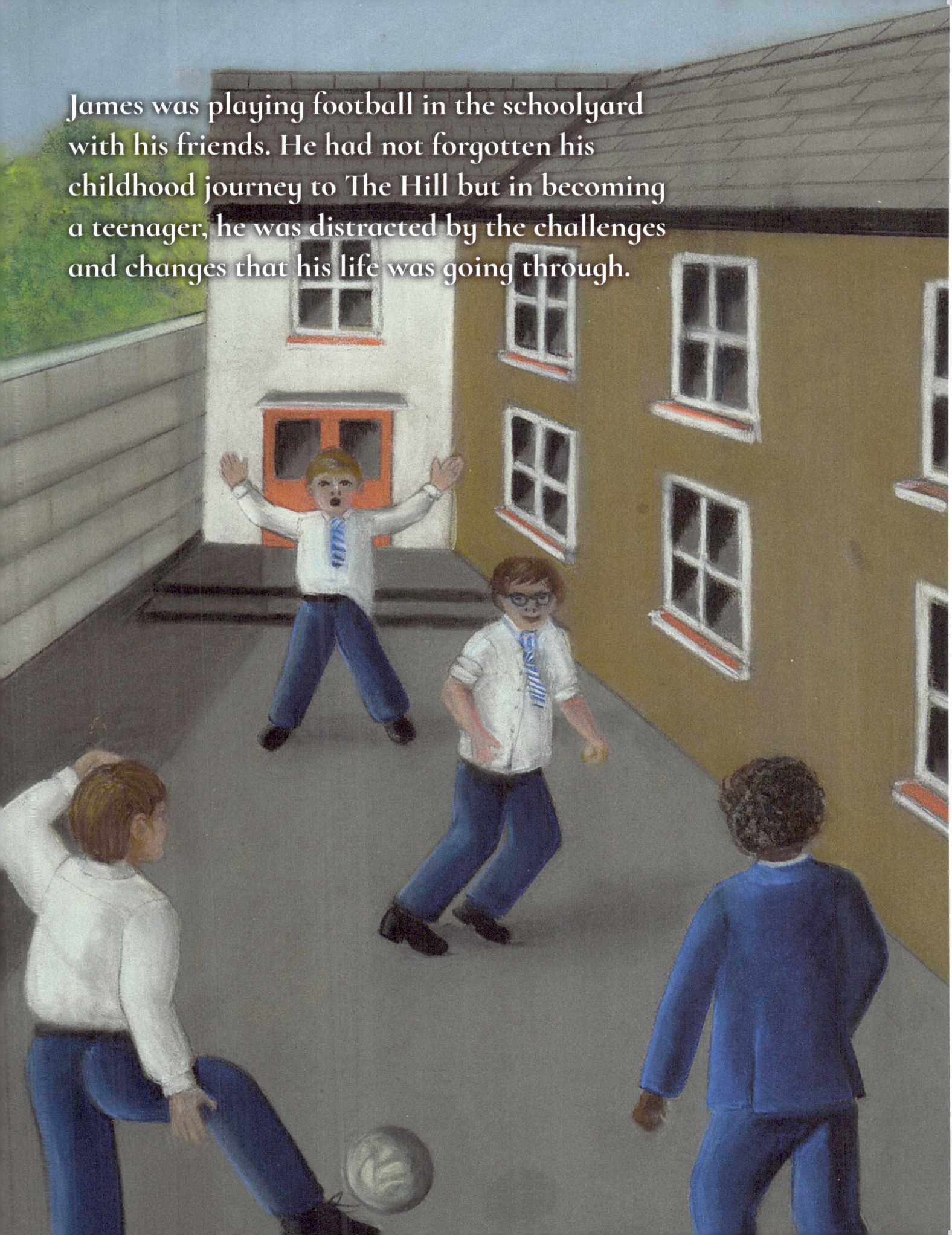

James was playing football in the schoolyard with his friends. He had not forgotten his childhood journey to The Hill but in becoming a teenager, he was distracted by the challenges and changes that his life was going through.

A teacher appears from the school doors and shouts his name, telling James that he is required to come to the school reception immediately. James begins his journey from the playground to the school reception office.

On entering through the door, all James can see is one long corridor, with a large set of stairs going down at one end, and a small set of stairs going up at the far end. James stops two steps down and realises that he is feeling fear about the unknown reason for going to reception.

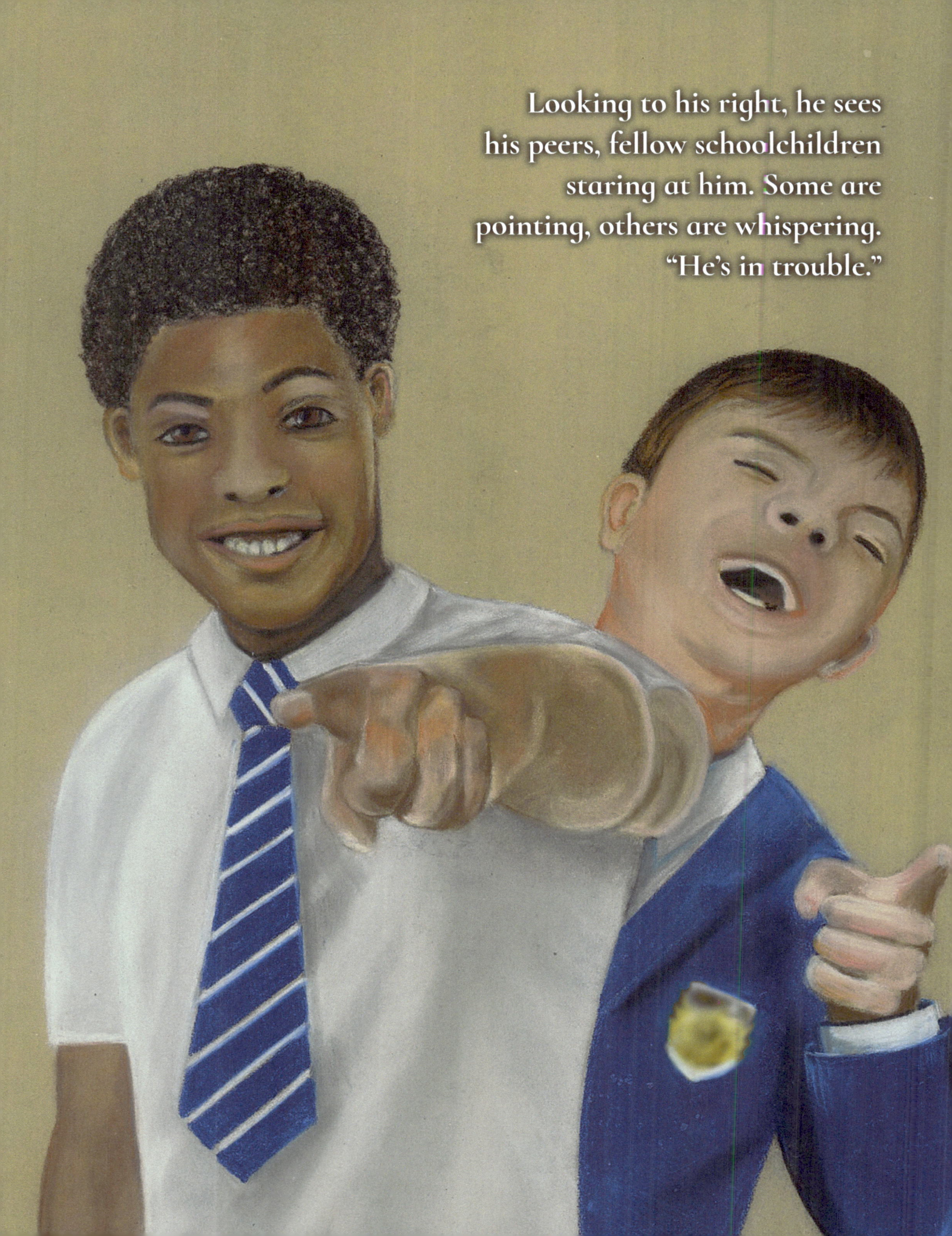

At the bottom of the staircase were two huge glass doors. Stood in front of those glass doors, was a teacher. James explains to the teacher that he'd been asked to go to reception, but the teacher would not let him past.

The teacher looked down on him, telling him that he wasn't good enough that he needed to try harder, that he wasn't going to make something of himself.

The teacher warns James that he cannot get to where he's in a rush to get to, without doing his homework in a certain way, by a certain time.

James sees no way of getting to reception, other than to push past the teacher.

Further along the corridor James encounters a careers advisor. The careers advisor blocks his path and tells him that he can't get to reception.

He had to get a job in a factory instead. Because if James isn't studying for university, he can forget ever having the successful life that waits for him at reception.

"Successful life", thinks James, "what on earth does that mean?"

As James progresses along the corridor, he encounters a man who owns a business.

The businessman blocks his path and tells him that he would never be worth a lot of money and that James needs to do exactly as he's told because he's not allowed to do things his own way.

James is told that he must conform, conform, conform.

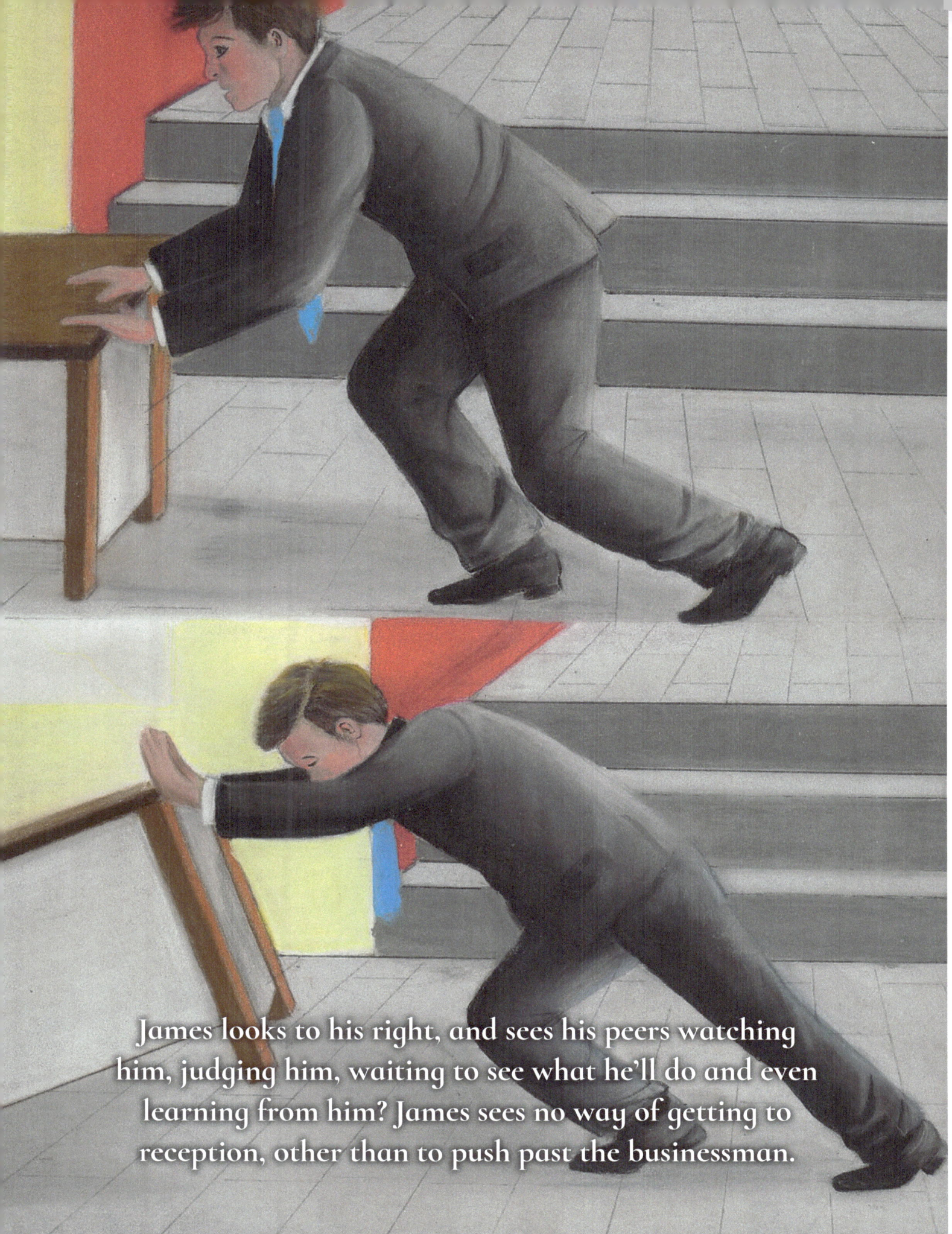

As James approaches the small staircase that rises towards the reception, his progress is stopped by one more blockage. This time, it isn't a person in his way, it's a voice in his head. The voice sternly questions:

"Are you sure you're good enough?"

"Are you sure you're doing the right thing?"

"Are you sure you're not making a huge mistake?"

"Are you sure you're going to get to the reception?"

"Are you sure you shouldn't just give up?"

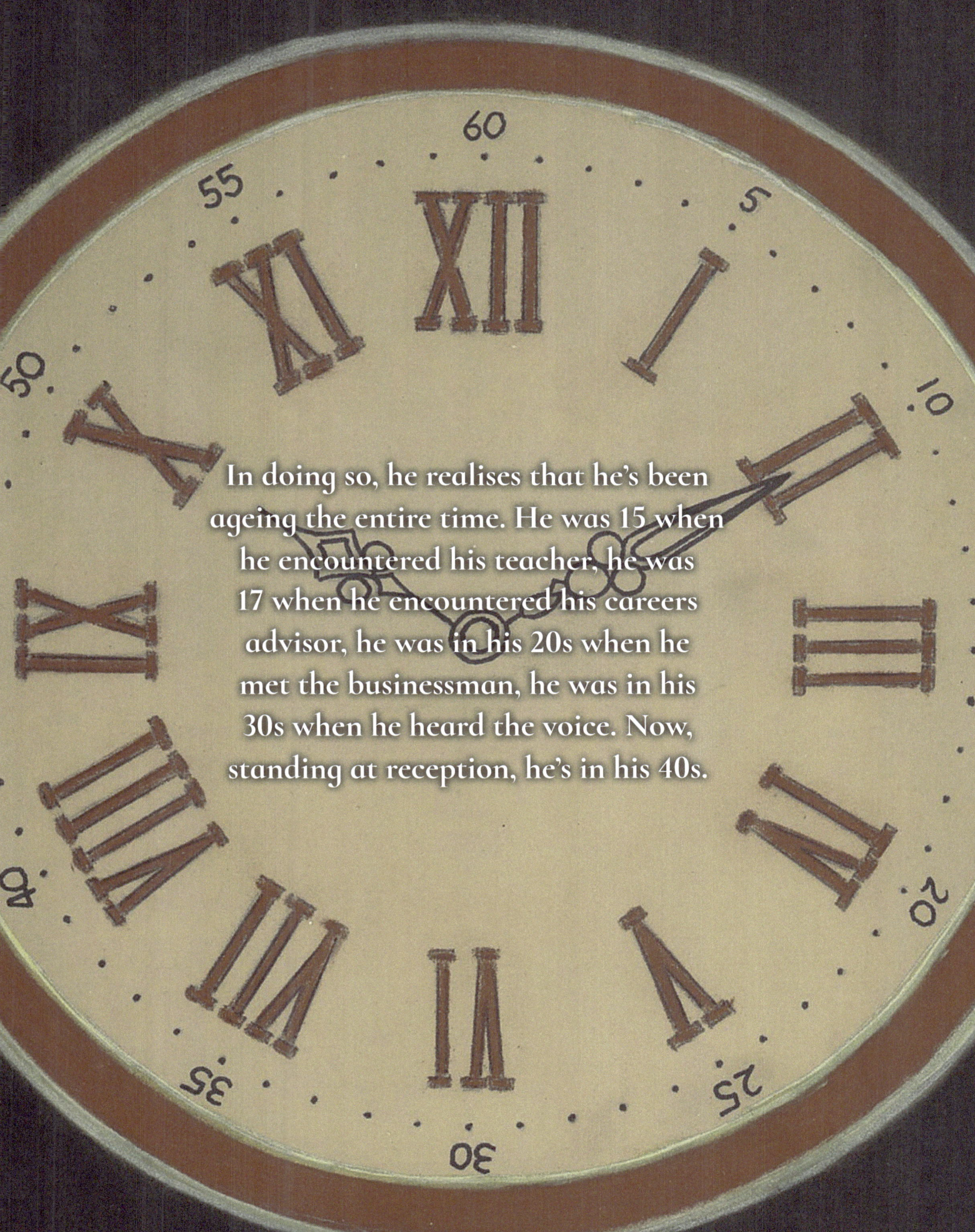

In doing so, he realises that he's been ageing the entire time. He was 15 when he encountered his teacher, he was 17 when he encountered his careers advisor, he was in his 20s when he met the businessman, he was in his 30s when he heard the voice. Now, standing at reception, he's in his 40s.

At reception, James' beautiful little daughter Grace is waiting for him. The little girl is young and innocent, and looks up with wide eyes towards her daddy. She wanted to see him to give him a big cuddle. That's the only reason she's there.

James bends down to hold her. James takes Grace into his arms and holds her as tightly as he possibly can.

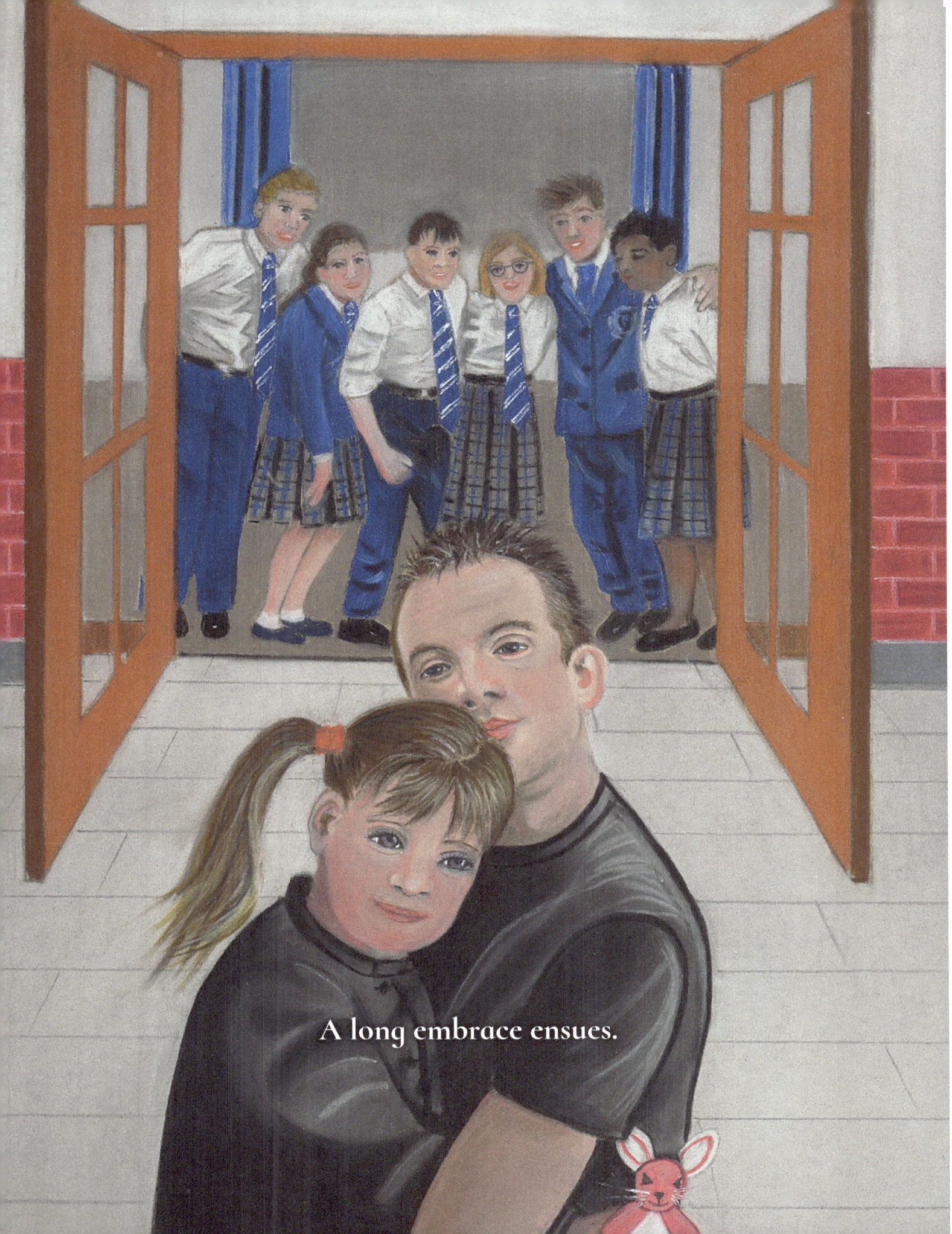

After a lengthy pause, James hears a voice. This time it's not the voice of a little girl, but rather, of a young woman. "Daddy, I'm ready now." James lets go of his girl.

His little girl is now a beautiful young woman in her high school uniform. Grace is ready to take on the very challenges that James has gone through.

James understands that we all need roots to strengthen us and wings to fly. James sees that he could never have helped to give his daughter roots or wings if he hadn't had to obtain them for himself. I understand that too.

And I understand that because of a
dream I had when I was 44 years old.

About the Author

Martin Bissett, aged 15, 30 and 44

About the Illustrator

Pamela Carter

Pam too had a dream, which was to pursue a career in paediatric physiotherapy.

When a back injury put paid to that, she retrained as a teacher of adults. A mini stroke struck in 2013 and Pam decided to go on a cruise as part of her recuperation. On the ship she joined an art class and the rest is history.

Since then Pam has delivered many commissions as she has refined her style in watercolour and pastels.

All profit from this book goes to support
The Upward Spiral Foundation.

Do you want to be a star in someone else's life? Scan the QR Code to purchase a Star mug, hoodie, t-shirt, cushion or other items in the shop. Each purchase helps the Upward Spiral Foundation's purpose to help people feel less helpless, hopeless and homeless.'

www.ingramcontent.com/pod-product-compliance
Lightning Source LLC
Chambersburg PA
CBHW042248100526

44587CB00002B/72